A BEGINNER'S GUIDE TO
COMPETITIVE
OBEDIENCE

WENDY BEASLEY

Dedication

To Alison Taylor, for many Friday training sessions, and
to Gemond Dell and Trevwen Taurus, who gave me
such success and pleasure in obedience competitions.

contents

Also by the same author : **A Beginners Guide To Working Trials**

Acknowledgements

I would like to thank Diane Ling
and her dogs Kenzie, Digger, Breeze, Kasba, Briar and Fern
for all their help with the photographs
and my husband Paul
for his patience in taking them.

INTRODUCTION

Some dogs cannot handle an idle life and, however much they are loved and pampered, they remain frustrated and bored. Unemployment can be as destructive for dogs as for people and can often lead to bad behaviour. Many such misunderstood dogs end up in rescue kennels or worse, but the lucky ones usually find their way to a training club with desperate but caring owners looking for a miracle cure. Although not quite a miracle, the transformation of these dogs when they start to learn is sometimes not far short of miraculous. It does not seem to matter what they learn – it is the fact that their minds are being stimulated that brings about the improvement.

Perhaps this sounds familiar to you, or perhaps your dog has not given

It's great to win prizes in obedience competition but the most important thing is that you and your dog enjoy competing.

you any problems because you have recognised its need to learn from the outset and now you are proud of its achievements. Either way, you may be ready to go one step further and try your luck at obedience competition. If you already belong to a training club and have taken part in club tests or matches in which you and your dog have done quite well, probably you have been 'bitten by the bug'. However, it is not always easy to know where to begin. For this reason, I hope to shed a little light on the mysteries of

Show day: a line-up of happy competitors and dogs at an Open show.

obedience competitions so that you may avoid some of the confusion and pitfalls that I encountered when I attempted to 'set the world on fire' with my first obedience dog, a very patient and forgiving Boxer!

All obedience competition in the United Kingdom is governed by The Kennel Club (KC) although in Scotland some authority is delegated to the Scottish Kennel Club. The Irish Kennel Club governs events in Southern Ireland but the awards under Irish Kennel Club Rules are not counted

towards United Kingdom qualifications or titles. Some smaller shows may be exempt from KC Rules but their organisers must still apply to The Kennel Club for a licence to hold an *exemption show*, and dogs entering such shows do not have to be registered with The Kennel Club. For all other shows held under KC Rules, dogs must be registered with The Kennel Club. For obedience purposes the dog need not be a pedigree and can be registered on the Obedience and Working Trials Register to ensure it complies with entry requirements. Registration forms can be obtained from The Kennel Club, and a small fee is payable. No details of your dog's background need be given for the Obedience and Working Trials Register but, if your dog is a pedigree and you wish it to be registered under its breed, both its parents must already be registered and other guarantees must be provided, such as the breeder's and stud dog owner's signatures. The breeder may already have registered the litter, but you must make sure you have transferred ownership into your own name, unless you are handling on the owner's behalf, or you will be in breach of KC Rules when you enter a show. If your dog has not been registered and you do not intend to breed or show, it is probably easier to apply only for obedience and working trial registration.

Dogs must be at least six months old to enter any obedience show but it is a good idea to go to a local show and watch some obedience competitions before taking part yourself. It is also a great help to join a local training club, where you will not only receive help and advice with your training but also meet other competitors and find out when and where the shows are held. Another advantage of joining a training club is that sooner or later you will probably get a chance to take part in club tests, which will give you a taste of competition. Your club may also enter matches with other clubs or belong to a league that holds regular inter-club rallies and, if you and your dog are good enough, you may be chosen to represent your club in competition. There is almost certainly a training club near you and, if you don't know where your nearest one is, you can find out from The Kennel Club, which keeps a list of all registered dog training clubs. You may also find it useful to subscribe to one of the canine journals which advertise forthcoming shows and, once you start competing, you will want to read reports and results from the shows, especially if you have done well. Several such magazines are available but, for obedience competition, *Dog Training Weekly* is the most comprehensive.

Exemption Shows

Exemption shows can offer the new competitor a taste of obedience competition, with the added advantage that they are entered on the day, so you do not need to decide weeks in advance whether your dog is ready. If you keep an eye on the dog papers you will see advertisements for exemption shows most weekends throughout the summer. Not all offer obedience classes, so you will need to ring up and ask for a schedule or details of classes. These shows do not need to conform to the usual KC classes and exercises may vary, but there are usually some very elementary classes with such titles as *Triers* or *Hopefuls* whose entry is restricted to absolute beginners. Although exemption shows cater for newcomers they also offer classes to suit experienced handlers bringing out new dogs, and the top class often attracts some very experienced Open and Championship handlers if there are no other shows that day. This can be very helpful as you will not only get a chance to work your own dog in show conditions but also be able to sit by the other rings and, by watching more experienced dogs and handlers being put through their paces, get an idea of the standard of Open competition.

As I said before, you do not need to enter these shows until the day and entries, which are usually very cheap, are taken from about an hour before judging starts. There may only be one class that suits you and your dog but, apart from watching the other obedience classes, you may like to take part in some of the novelty classes, such as *Dog in best condition* or *Dog with the waggiest tail*. Exemption shows can really be great fun and wonderful training grounds, getting you and your dog used to a show atmosphere with noise, people and other dogs.

Limited shows

One step up from the exemption show is the Limited show, where entries are restricted by various means, sometimes to an area or, again, to members of the Society holding the show. More often though they are limited to dogs of one breed and held in conjunction with breed showing classes. Awards gained at either these or exemption shows do not count towards qualification for Open or Championship classes. However, they do offer the new competitor ring experience and, if there is one in your area and you are eligible, it is well worth entering, as the classes are often smaller and less competitive than at the larger shows.

Open and Championship Shows

In obedience competition there is very little difference between Open and Championship shows until you reach the top class. At Championship shows Obedience Certificates (OCs) are awarded, and these count towards the title Obedience Champion on offer for the winners of the Championship C Classes (Dog and Bitch), but the other classes remain the same. Winners of OCs, often referred to by competitors as *tickets*, qualify for entry at The Kennel Club Obedience Championships, which take place annually at Crufts. Winners of three tickets under three different judges are awarded the title of Obedience Champion, provided that they have gained at least 285 points out of a possible 300 points.

Entering a Show

When you find a show in your area you will need to obtain a schedule well in advance and send in your entry before the closing date, which is normally a month to six weeks before the show. The schedule will come complete with entry form and, although this may appear somewhat daunting, I will explain it more fully once we've established what you're entering!

Obedience shows are split into classes. At Limited and Open shows, Pre-Beginners may be scheduled as well as the usual Beginners, Novice, and Classes A, B and C. At Championship shows in addition to the usual classes two Championship Class Cs (one for dogs and one for bitches) will be scheduled, and Obedience Certificates (OCs) awarded to the winners, provided that they have not lost more than 15 marks in total. These classes consist of a number of set exercises increasing in difficulty from the very basic Pre-Beginners to the highly advanced Class C. I will go into detail about each exercise and its requirements later, but for now I will just explain the classes.

Pre-Beginners

This class caters for the absolute beginner, the owner, handler or dog must not have won a first prize in Pre-Beginners or been placed third or above in any higher obedience class. The exercises in this class are very elementary and handlers may encourage their dogs verbally and use as many commands as they like in any exercises other than the stay tests. Physical correction and encouragement by means of using the lead or touching the dog is not permitted during exercises. The exercises and total marks available are:

Heel on lead	15
Heel free	20
Recall	10
Sit for one minute	10
Down for two minutes	20
Total	**75**

Beginners

Although this class is also designed for the beginner it is possible to continue competing at this level until two wins are obtained in Beginners or one win in any higher class. Once again, dogs may be encouraged or commanded verbally but no handling is permitted during tests and no extra commands or signals may be given during the stay exercises. In both Pre-Beginners and Beginners the judge may allow handlers to face their dogs during stays. The exercises and marks for the Beginners class are:

Heel on lead	15
Heel free	20
Recall	10
Retrieve any article	25
Sit for one minute	10
Down for two minutes	20
Total	**100**

Novice

This class is aimed not so much at the new handler as at the new dog. The ruling in the first two classes prevents entry by people, either owners or handlers, who have won previously with a different dog. However, in Novice it is only the dog that is considered, which means that experienced handlers with young dogs can enter and continue to work in Novice until they have been awarded two first prizes in any obedience class, with the exception of Pre-Beginners and Beginners. Once again, verbal encouragement is permitted and there is no limit on extra commands except in the stay tests, but touching the dog or use of the lead during exercises will be penalised. Once again, at the judge's discretion, handlers may be permitted to face their dogs in the stay exercises. In this class the exercises and marks are as follows:

Temperament Test	10
Heel on lead	15
Heel free	20
Recall	10
Retrieve a dumbbell	15
Sit for one minute	10
Down for two minutes	20
Total	**100**

Class A

The step between Novice and Class A is a big one, as in this class no extra commands are allowed, and the scent test and out of sight stay are introduced. Class A is open to dogs who have not won three first prizes in Classes A, B or C and, although simultaneous command and signal are permitted, any extra commands or signals will be penalised. Although handlers remain in sight with their backs to their dogs during the sit stay, they go out of the dog's sight for the down stay, which lasts for five minutes. Most handlers do not attempt this or any higher class until they and their dogs have considerable experience and confidence in the lower classes. The exercises and marks for Class A are as follows:

Heel on lead 15
Heel free 25
Recall A 15
Retrieve a dumbbell 25
Sit two minutes (handler in sight) 10
Down five minutes (handler out of sight) 30
Scent discrimination (handler's scent – no decoy) 30
Total **150**

Class B

This is for dogs who have not won three or more first prizes in either Class B or C. Only one command by word or signal is allowed except in the sendaway, where the dog may be sent with a simultaneous command and signal. All heelwork is performed off the lead with the dog and handler being tested at normal slow and fast pace. New exercises are introduced, including the sendaway and stand stay, and the retrieve article is provided by the judge. Exercises and marks are as follows:

Heel free 40
Sendaway, drop and recall 40
Retrieve judge's article 30
Stand stay for one minute, handler in sight 10
Sit stay for two minutes, handler out of sight 20
Down stay for five minutes, handler out of sight 30
Scent discrimination (handler's scent with one decoy) 30
Total **200**

Class C (Open and Championship)

Class C, whether Open or Championship, calls for the greatest level of skill from both dog and handler. The exercises are challenging and absolute accuracy is essential. At Open level this class is open to all dogs and handlers but at Championship level the dog must have qualified for entry by winning out of Classes Novice, A and B as well as winning Open Class C on at least one occasion, having been placed no lower than third on three other occasions. The Open Class C win and Open Class C places must be under different judges. In both Open and Championship classes all exercises are carried out off the lead and no extra commands are permitted other than to send the dog in the sendaway, drop and recall exercise, where a simultaneous command and signal may be used. Exercises and marks are:

Heelwork, including normal fast and slow pace and positions
on the move 60
Sendaway, drop and recall 40
Retrieve judge's article...30
Distant control..50
Sit stay for two minutes, handler out of sight 20
Down stay for 10 minutes, handler out of sight 50
Scent discrimination (judge's scent with decoy or decoys) 50
Total **300**

General Remarks

The maximum number of dogs allowed to compete in any obedience class is 60 and, with the exception of Championship Class C, if the entry exceeds 60 the class must be divided into equal sections with each section judged by a separate judge. In Championship classes, if the entry exceeds 60 numbers are reduced by a ballot based on points awarded previously to competitors for wins and places in Open and Championship Class C.

NAME OF SOCIETY NUMBER OF CLASSES OPEN/CHAMPIONSHIP OBEDIENCE SHOW held under Kennel Club Rules and Show Regulations	ENTRY FEES: CATALOGUE: NOT FOR COMPETITION:
INSTRUCTIONS for filling in form and Kennel Club requirements for entry	CHEQUES PAYABLE TO: CLOSING DATE:

	Registered Name of Dog	Breed	Sex D or B	Full Date of Birth	Breeder	SIRE (BLOCK LETTERS)	DAM (BLOCK LETTERS)	To be entered in Classes numbered

DECLARATION stating that you agree to be bound by Kennel Club Rules and Regulations and that your dog is eligible for entry and not liable to disqualification. You must also sign to say the dog is free from any contagious or infectious disease and is in good health and that if the dog becomes infected or is in contact with any infectious or contagious disease within 21 days of the show you will withdraw from competition.

Signed................................ Date................................

NOTE-Dogs entered in breach of Kennel Club Show Regulations are liable to disqualification whether or not the owner was aware of the breach.

Name of Owner (Mr Mrs Miss) . . . .
Address . . . .
. . . .
. . . .
Telephone . . . .

ENTRIES AND FEES TO:

Typical entry form for an obedience competition.

EXEMPTION DOG SHOW
(By kind permission of The Kennel Club)
(Dogs need not be registered with The Kennel Club)
IN AID OF

DATE
ENTRIES TAKEN FROM **JUDGING STARTS AT**
Entry fees: per class

Classes 1–4 for pedigree dogs only – Judge:
1 Any Variety (AV) Puppy (6–12 months)
2 AV Sporting
3 AV Non-Sporting
4 AV Open

Classes 5–15 Open to all dogs – Judge:
5 AV Crossbreed
6 AV Veteran
7 Best Rescued Dog
8 Best Local Dog
9 Dog in Best Condition
10 Dog the Judge Would Most Like to Take Home
11 Dog with the Waggiest Tail
12 Dog and Owner Most Alike
13 AV Brace
14 Happy Families
15 Best Party Trick

**ROSETTES TO SIXTH PLACE, TROPHY FOR BEST PEDIGREE AND
BEST NOVELTY TAKEN FROM ALL CLASS WINNERS**

OBEDIENCE CLASSES

Class 16 Starters – Judge:
Open to dogs and handlers never having been placed in any obedience show. Heel on lead; Recall (no finish); Sit half a minute; Down one minute (both in sight).

Class 17 Improvers – Judge:
Open to dogs that have not won more than one first place in Novice at an Open Show. Heel on lead; heel free; Novice Recall; Retrieve a dumbbell; Sit one minute; Down two minutes (both in sight).

Class 17 High Flyers – Judge:
Open to dogs that have not been placed in Class A or higher at Open Shows – no extra commands. Heel free, Recall to heel; Retrieve a dumbbell, Test A scent; Sit two minutes; Down four minutes (both out of sight).

Typical schedule for an Exemption show.

All these classes are designed to give competitors a steady route through to Class C, allowing them time to perfect each exercise before moving on to the next class. Each test is a stepping stone to the next and, if you keep a 'blueprint' of each class in your mind, you will be able to train each exercise with a view to progression through the classes.

I am grateful to the *Kennel Club Year Book 1996/97* for verification of this information, but both classes and qualifications are subject to alteration and, although correct at time of writing, the information should be checked in the current Year Book's 'Rules and Regulations' section before entry.

HEELWORK, TEMPERAMENT TEST, ASSD

Heelwork

Competitive obedience amounts to no more than seven exercises, which increase in difficulty according to the class. The first and arguably the most important of these exercises is heelwork. Until this skill is mastered to a reasonably high standard, progress beyond the lower classes is unlikely and the more advanced exercises will be irrelevant.

Heelwork: ready to start.

My own introduction to the intricacies of competitive heelwork was at a local training club where a rather formidable lady yelled military style commands to an odd selection of people and an even odder selection of dogs. As we followed each other round in a large circle, wrestling with our over-exuberant or just-plain-awkward canine companions, we were periodically ordered to 'do our corners'. Unfortunately, none of us had any idea what she was talking about and, as we were more intent on preventing our dogs from biting each other, tripping us up, or strangling themselves, we were probably not giving her our full attention. Needless to say, I certainly cannot remember any corners being 'done'! However, as the weeks went by and the dogs became less excited, I began to listen and take notice of this surprisingly knowledgeable lady and, gradually, it began to make sense. I realised that 'doing corners' meant turning smartly at right angles and not 'wheeling' – I was making progress! My Boxer bitch and subsequently her daughter were soon giving impressive performances at club and exemption show level and my first Border Collie bitch progressed

Heelwork: attentive heelwork.

as far as Class B in Open competition – and this in spite of my lack of appreciation for a dog who watched its handler, causing me to try constantly to persuade her to 'look where she was going'!

Competitive heelwork is not practical; it is more like a dressage test, the emphasis being on concentration and accuracy. In Pre-Beginners, Beginners, Novice and Class A the heelwork is performed both on and off lead, but this does not mean the lead can be used to guide or correct the dog, and any tension on the lead will be penalised. Heelwork both on and off the lead commences with the dog sitting on the left side of the handler. When asked to move forward the handler should command the dog and move off smartly, the dog adopting the heelwork position, and both should continue walking as directed by the steward. The judge will be looking for an attentive dog who maintains a constant position on the handler's left side without drifting wide or impeding progress. The dog's shoulder should be approximately level with the handler's leg and at no time should the dog surge forward or lag behind. Many dogs naturally carry their heads turned towards their handler and this enables them to anticipate any change of direction or halt. However, this is not a requirement, and a dog should not be penalised for looking straight ahead if it executes the turns and halts neatly without error. The Kennel Club Rules call for a dog to work in a happy, natural manner but this means different things for different breeds – can you imagine a Bloodhound or a Shar Pei looking happy? A good judge will take this into consideration when marking the exercise.

Heelwork: tight about turn.

The judge in each class will plan the heelwork test and inform the steward of the pattern. It is then up to the steward to issue instructions to the handler, leaving the judge free to mark the exercise. These instructions can include halts and turns as well as changes of pace. The lower the class the more straightforward the pattern and, in Pre-Beginners and Beginners,

Heelwork: sitting on halt.

only left, right and right about turns are allowed. In Novice and Class A, handlers may be instructed to make a diagonal turn and, in Class B, left about turns may be introduced. In Class C the judge may ask for figures-of-eight, weaving or circles, and it is not uncommon to be instructed to execute a multiple turn in one direction (for instance, a double about turn or a right about turn – right turn, or left about turn – left turn). However, these multiple turns can only be given singly and should be followed by a stretch of heelwork with no turns.

The changes of pace in Class B are from a halt but, in Class C normal, fast and slow pace can be asked for at any time during heelwork and marks will be lost for slow, untidy or unconvincing transitions. The three paces in heelwork should be noticeably different, and handlers often lose marks for indefinable changes. Turns at all paces should be executed smartly on command from the steward, and handlers may be penalised for walking on or hesitating after an instruction. The dog should remain at the heel position throughout the turn, and wide right or about turns and kneeing the dog on a left or left about will all be penalised. When the handler is instructed to halt, marks can be lost once again for significant walking on or hesitation. As the handler halts, the dog should sit squarely at the left side in a straight line with its shoulder level with the handler's leg. In Pre-Beginners, Beginners and Novice the handler may command the dog to sit but, in the higher classes, where no extra commands are permitted, the dog is expected to assume the correct sit position without being told when the handler halts. Similarly, encouragement and correction can be given verbally in the lower classes but, in Class A or above, the dog is only commanded at the start of the exercise or following a halt; no other encouragement or correction is permitted.

In Class C the judge will sometimes set out poles, bollards or other such markers for the heelwork and dog and handler may have to perform a figure-of-eight or weave around these obstacles. Here again, the emphasis will be on accuracy, with the dog maintaining the heel position throughout the manoeuvre and the judge marking accordingly.

Advanced Stand, Sit and Down (ASSD)

Again in Class C, as well as being tested at all three paces, the dog will be required to stop on command and remain in a sit, stand or down position while the handler continues to walk forward. This exercise is known as the ASSD, and the judge decides where and in what order the three positions are required, which must be the same for all dogs. The handler will be warned by a steward when a position is imminent and will then be

ASSD: stand.

instructed to command the dog. Usually, the handler is issued with a card printed with the order of positions at the beginning of heelwork and the steward will then say something like, 'First position coming... now.'

Sometimes a judge will set markers in the ring with the positions displayed and the dog will be given the command as the handler passes each marker. Judges have their own variations on this exercise but the end result remains much the same. The dog will be required to stay in one position whilst the handler walks on as directed by the steward until reaching the dog again, when both will continue forward, resuming normal heelwork. Marks can be lost here for extra commands, missed positions, hesitation by dog or handler or movement by the dog when left, so training for this exercise needs to be thorough.

That is the basis of heelwork and, to achieve the best results, the exercise must be thoroughly taught so that it is performed exactly the same on or off the lead. Although changes of pace and ASSD make the test more complicated, sound training of the correct heelwork position will ensure that the dog will strive to maintain it throughout any manoeuvre. I cannot stress too strongly how important this exercise is, as it forms the basis of all obedience competition, and many top obedience handlers will assess a dog's working potential by its aptitude for heelwork.

Temperament Test

In the Novice class, before heel on lead commences, the dog is tested for temperament. Most dogs need very little training for this exercise, which

ASSD: sit.

just consists of the judge approaching the dog as it stands beside its handler on the lead and running his or her hand down its back. The judge may speak to the dog but will not attempt to surprise or frighten it and the handler may also speak to the dog to reassure it. The test is marked out of 10, and the dog will lose marks for cringing, backing away or showing aggression. However, if your dog has been well socialised, this should not present any problem, and too much emphasis on this test in training can sometimes worry the dog and create a problem where there wasn't one. Unless your dog is unduly nervous or aggressive it will probably quite enjoy this exercise.

ASSD: down.

RECALL AND RETRIEVE

The Recall

It would be a wonderful world if all dogs came when they were called. Sadly many do not, and those that do usually come in their own good time. While this might be satisfactory in a pet, the recall for an obedience exercise is a little more demanding. Depending on the class, the dog will either be required to come and sit in front of its stationary handler or to be recalled to heel whilst the handler is walking. Once again, this exercise must be taught thoroughly, as an accurate recall can make the difference between winning and losing in any class.

Pre-Beginners, Beginners and Novice

In Pre-Beginners, Beginners and Novice, the recall exercise is much the same, although distances may vary. Handlers will be directed to a place in the ring and asked to put their dogs in either the sit or the down position; their choice. They will be asked by the steward if they are ready and then will be instructed to command their dogs using whatever words they choose. In these classes the steward will not say 'Last command,' as the handlers are at liberty to go on commanding their dogs throughout the exercise. They will then be instructed to leave their dogs and should walk away from them in a straight line until told to about turn and halt. If the handlers have managed to walk straight this manoeuvre will bring them directly in line with and facing their dog. However, many beginner handlers are horrified to see that, when they turn to face their dogs, they are not actually in line at all – more off at a tangent! This is where you may see some shifty shuffling from the handlers and inexperienced dogs doing their best to straighten up from a diagonal approach. More experienced handlers have learned to focus on something directly in front when they leave their dogs so that they walk a straight line and, just in case their dogs can't walk straight, they teach their dogs to sit squarely in front from any angle.

When the handler reaches the designated spot, he or she will be asked to call the dog, and this can be by word, signal or both, and as many times as they like. The dog, who should have remained in position until this point, should come immediately when called, arrive in front of the handler and sit straight in line with the handler's legs. All this can be assisted in these classes by verbal encouragement, hand signals and even a certain amount of body movement as long as the handler's feet do not move and he doesn't touch his dog. However, it is wise to aim for an unassisted recall; in

Recall: happy recall.

Recall: dog waits for call.

the higher classes no extra commands or body signals are permitted, so the dog should not learn to rely on them. In my experience, no amount of swaying around or arm waving really helps the dog, although it may make the handler feel better. If the dog has been taught this position (the *present*) correctly from day one and has always been praised in that position it will do its utmost to earn its reward.

The conclusion of this test is the return to heel, and this can be done in one of two ways. Either the dog will move from facing the handler to its left and round behind the handler, arriving at the handler's left hand side in the heel position and sit; or the dog can perform the continental style finish where, from the front, he moves to his right and turns a small anti-clockwise circle at the handler's left hand side, finishing once again in the heel position at the sit. Either of these finishes is

Recall: present.

Recall: finish to heel.

acceptable as long as it is neat and smooth. The first is probably easier for the dog to perform, especially if it is a long-backed breed, but the second can look much more impressive if done well.

The Beginner/Novice Recall therefore consists of four different stages, and the experienced handler will teach them all quite separately.

1 The *stay* or *wait*, which should be 100% steady before moving on.
2 The *call up* which should, at the very least, be smart if not fast, as marks will be lost for any hesitation, wandering, sniffing or stopping on route.
3 The *sit in front*, which can be split again so the dog is taught to present from any angle from perhaps no more than two or three paces away. This training will prove its worth on the odd occasion when the judge asks for a diagonal recall.
4 The *finish to heel*, which many handlers find easier to teach on the lead to ensure that the dog remains close to the handler's legs or executes a tight circle and does not wander or lose concentration.

All this can be brought together when each part has been perfected and the dog is reliable in all stages.

Classes A, B and C

In Class A the dog is once again left in the sit or down position at the handler's choice, but is recalled whilst the handler is walking away from the dog, and the dog must assume the heel position and continue walking until the handler halts. The Class B and C recalls follow the sendaway and the dog is recalled from the sendaway point to join the walking handler and once again assumes the heel position, sitting when the handler halts. This type of recall still needs to be broken down and taught thoroughly, making sure that the dog will stay whilst the handler walks about and come immediately when called. The dog can be taught to drop into the heel position from any angle of approach, once again from just a few paces away, using the lead if necessary, and the accurate sit should be easy if it has been well taught during heelwork training. In this exercise, whether in A, B or C, the judge will be looking for a dog who comes immediately it is called, but not before, with no creeping or anticipation. It should join the handler quickly by the shortest possible route and immediately match its pace to the handler's with no overshooting or lagging behind. It will also be penalised for a crooked sit or failure to sit at the halt, and the handler will be marked for waiting for the dog, body signals or extra commands.

A Recall: dog about to be recalled.

A Recall: dog moves forward to join handler.

A Recall: dog arrives smartly at heel.

A Recall: dog and handler continue forward as directed.

The Retrieve

The retrieve is probably one of the most natural things for a dog to do, and yet it is often one of the hardest exercises to teach and even harder to perfect. In obedience competition the retrieve is not a game; it is a job of work and, although many people teach the exercise with a toy, moving on to a dumbbell later, most experienced handlers feel this is avoiding the issue and prefer to introduce the dumbbell from the beginning. The object of the exercise is for the dog to wait at heel while the handler throws the retrieve article and commands the dog to retrieve. The dog should move smartly

Retrieve: presenting the dumbbell.

out, pick up the article cleanly with no chewing, mouthing or dropping, and return directly to the handler, sit in front and present the article. The dog must continue to hold the article without mouthing until the handler, commanded by the steward, takes it. The dog will then be sent to heel by the handler on the steward's command.

In Beginner classes the retrieve may be anything provided by the handler, and it is not unusual for toys or balls to be seen in this class. For Novice and A, the dog must retrieve a dumbbell, once again provided by the handler, and in B and C the judge will provide the retrieve article. This can be just about anything other than food, glass or something injurious to the dog, as long as it is clearly visible and easily picked up by any breed. Once again, although dogs may be verbally encouraged in Beginners and Novice, extra commands in Classes A, B, and C will be penalised.

Handlers who decide to teach this exercise with a toy and rely on the dog's enthusiasm to retrieve may come unstuck in the higher classes when the dog is faced with an article that it doesn't want to pick up. Judges set out to test the dogs, so they often choose retrieve articles that are awkward or less attractive and, if the exercise has not been taught as a discipline, the dog may not want to 'play' that day. Like all the other exercises, this one should be broken down for training purposes, and the first and most important lesson that the dog can learn is the hold. This command must be obeyed consistently no matter what the article and, once the dog will pick up and hold anything and everything without mouthing, you have the basis of a reliable retrieve. The rest of the exercise can be perfected through recall training as the return, present and finish are exactly the same.

Time spent perfecting this exercise in the early stages will prove its worth in scent discrimination tests later.

Retrieve: get your dog used to unusual retrieve items.

SCENT AND STAYS

Scent

Probably more tickets are won and lost on the scent test than any other exercise. Even from its introduction in Class A there are 30 marks to be lost and, by the time it gets to Class C, 50 marks are allocated to this single exercise. Many handlers dread it and even the most experienced have learned not to take scent for granted. It is probably our own lack of understanding of the dog's ability that causes the greatest problem, together with the assumption that this test can be 'taught', whereas the dog already knows how to use its nose.

Scent Cloths

Scent is introduced in Class A and at this level it is designed to encourage the dog. In all classes the test is carried out on cloths, which are usually (but do not have to be) white. At outdoor shows the cloths are weighted to prevent them from blowing about. This can take the dog by surprise if it has been taught on unweighted cloths, so it is wise to practise with both if you can.

Class A

In Class A six cloths are put out in a straight line, including one scented by the handler, and there are no decoys. The dog must go out, select the handler's cloth, and return to present and finish, all with no extra commands or encouragement. Scent is usually carried out separately from the other exercises, after all the dogs have completed the main ringwork. When called in to carry out the scent test, the handler and dog go to an allotted spot and the dog is faced away from the cloths. Usually the

Scent: finding the correct cloth.

Scent: the pick up.

Scent: returning smartly.

handlers have picked up a neutral cloth as they enter the ring and they are allowed time to hold and scent it. The handler then gives the cloth to the steward, who should use tongs or polythene gloves to take it and place it in the line in a space left among the other five blank cloths, which must be between 3ft and 5ft (0.9m and 2.5m) apart. Although in Class A the cloths must be laid in a straight line, the judge will decide whether the line is to be horizontal, vertical or diagonal and where in the line the handler's cloth will be placed. On the steward's command the handler will bring the dog to heel, facing the cloths, and indicate to the steward that they are ready. Then, again on steward's command, the handler will send the dog out to

Scent: presenting.

find the correct cloth, standing up straight before sending the dog. Handlers are allowed to 'give the dog scent' before sending, allowing the dog to sniff their hands or, in Class C, an extra cloth provided by the judge. It is doubtful if this is necessary in the case of the handler's own scent but it serves as a set-up procedure and probably makes the handler feel better.

Class B

In Class B the scent test may consist of up to ten cloths, but not less than six, which again must be laid 3–5ft (0.9–2.5m) apart. They need not be laid in a straight line and the judge can decide on the pattern but there should be one decoy among the cloths. Decoys are cloths that have been held by a decoy steward for the same amount of time as the handler has held his or hers. Both are then laid in the pattern at the same time by two stewards, in positions decided by the judge. The procedure for handler and dog is the same as for Class A and, once again, the dog should bring in the correct cloth and present it, finishing at heel, with no extra commands or signals.

Class C

Scent in Class C is considerably more difficult than in the other two classes in that the dog is not required to find the familiar scent of its handler (which should be easily recognisable, even in the presence of decoys) but that of the judge, on a cloth among blanks and at least one decoy. In this case the decoy or decoys will be held by the steward(s) for the same amount of time as the judge holds his or hers and put into the pattern at the same time. A minimum of six and a maximum of ten cloths, including the judge's and decoy or decoys, will be laid in a pattern decided by the judge. Obviously, it is vital in this case for the dog to sample the judge's unfamiliar scent before it is sent so that it can distinguish this cloth from the decoys. This exercise truly tests a dog's ability to discriminate between different scents but, although to us it would seem an impossible task, a confident, relaxed dog appears to have no difficulty. However, perhaps because of their own lack of confidence, many handlers manage to instil confusion and a fear of being wrong in their dogs when it comes to scent. This can be seen in dogs grabbing wildly at any or all of the cloths, refusing to pick up anything, or being unwilling to return to the handler when the choice has been made. To prevent these faults occurring in your dog it is necessary to introduce scent training gradually, with a great deal of praise and no criticism. The dog cannot read your mind, and *its* failure to understand is *your* failure to impart – not disobedience. There is no doubt that any dog of any breed can do the scent test if it understands what is required. If mistakes are made they are probably due to a communication problem rather than a lack of ability on the dog's part.

Marking

Marking scent tests in all classes is usually very harsh. Bringing in the wrong cloth results in all marks lost, and marks will be deducted for anticipation, mouthing or picking up the wrong cloth, mouthing or dropping the correct cloth at any time and extra commands (which, if over the cloths, can result in all marks lost), as well as the usual crooked present or crooked finish. Once again, thorough training in recall and retrieve help in this exercise and prevent needless marks from being lost for silly inaccuracies when the dog has done an otherwise good scent. Most handlers would agree that it is not wise to correct crooked sits or mouthing when practising scent. It is probably best to address these problems by way of extra present and hold lessons away from cloths, or the dog can become anxious over scent when it is really the recall or retrieve at fault. Despite the importance of this exercise, the handler who can treat it as just another test and convey this to the dog will probably have the most consistent results.

Stays

Stays are another set of exercises that carry heavy penalties for mistakes. Again, these are graduated in difficulty according to the class, but the dog who has thoroughly understood the principle of stay for one minute will stay for ten, so again it is the grounding that counts. In Pre-Beginners, Beginners and sometimes Novice classes the judge may decide to allow handlers to face their dogs during the stay tests but, for any handler aspiring to the higher classes, it makes more sense to teach your dog to stay when you are not looking at it, so it is best even in Pre-Beginners at least to stand sideways, if not with your back to your dog, as you will have to in higher classes.

Stay tests may take place in a separate 'stay ring' or in the ring in which the relevant class is being judged. Usually the times for the stay tests for each class are decided before the class commences and displayed on a notice board at the show or at the ringside. Sometimes, however, the judge will be allowed to decide when the stays should be and, in this case, they are more commonly held at the end of the class. This is usually the case at exemption shows. All stays are performed as a group exercise, and it is up to the handlers in each class to congregate for stays at the appropriate time and ring. The judge or steward will tell competitors where to stand, note their numbers and sometimes their dog's breed and name and usually tell them how the test should be carried out. It is very important to listen carefully to these instructions, which often include such things as where to stand during the stays and where the 'out of sight' is to be. In all stay exercises the steward will give a 'last command' instruction, and any commands after that will be penalised. At the end of each stay test the steward will say, 'Exercise finished,' and only then should the handler release and praise his or her dog.

In Pre-Beginners, Beginners and Novice the length of stays are the same: one minute sit and two minutes down, both with the handler in sight. The judge may decide to carry out the tests in any order, although it is more usual to do the sit followed by the down. Handlers will be given time to settle their dogs in each position and then will be told to give their last command and leave their dogs. They should then immediately walk away from their dogs to wherever the steward or judge directs and remain without speaking, moving or signalling until told to return to their dogs. As mentioned previously, in these classes handlers may be allowed to face their dogs if they wish, but they will briefed before the exercise commences.

In Class A the times increase to two minutes sit with the handler in sight and an out-of-sight down stay lasting five minutes. In the sit exercise, handlers stand with their backs to their dogs and in the down they will be instructed to leave their dogs and walk to a place out of sight until called to return to the ring. In Class B the stand stay is introduced and, although handlers do not go out of sight, this can still be quite a difficult test. Very few dogs are happy in the stand position, which is a very dominant pose to adopt amongst other dogs, especially when their handlers are on the other

Stay: the sit stay.

side of the ring. However, patience in teaching this test can pay off and result in a confident, happy dog who is not worried about being left. In Classes B and C, both the sit and the down stays are out of sight, the sit for two minutes and the down for five in Class B and ten in Class C. However, as I said at the beginning, if the stay has been well taught, time has no relevance to the dog, who will be confident of the handler's eventual return. For this reason, training for the stays should be based on absolute steadiness in all three positions for just a short time. When the exercise is fully understood it will not be difficult to increase the time or go out of sight. To the well taught dog, 'Stay' means 'Stay', regardless of what the handler or anyone else is doing.

Stay: the down stay.

This Beardie clearly enjoys the sit stay

SENDAWAY AND DISTANT CONTROL

Two of the more advanced exercises in obedience competition are sendaway and distant control. Both involve the dog working away from the handler, which requires confidence and an assurance of being right. Dogs who have been bullied in either of these exercises will show their anxiety and perform badly but, if the handler has taken the time to ensure the dog understands the exercises, results in these particular tests can be quite spectacular.

The Sendaway

In the sendaway exercise the handler will be directed to a place in the ring from where the dog will be sent, on command from steward to handler, in a direction and to a point indicated by the judge or steward. On reaching the point the dog must drop into the down position on command and remain down until called by the handler. As in Class A recall, the dog will be called whilst the handler is walking where directed by the steward, and the dog must join the handler by the most direct route, continuing at heel and sitting when the handler halts. If the dog has reached a good standard of Class A recall this part of the test will not need to be taught. The same

Sendaway: setting up for the sendaway.

Sendaway: heading for the box.

criteria for marking will be used and the same faults penalised, so the good Class A recall will be a good Class B or C recall. The sendaway point is usually marked in some way and could be anything from a single post to a four-

Sendaway: good positioning in the box.

cornered box marked with road cones or a triangle marked with tape on the ground. I have even seen four Easter bonnets or a decoy duck marking the spot! However, there is no obligation to put out markers, and some judges will just ask for the dog to be sent to the corner of the ring, a knot in the ring ropes, or a patch of daisies. There are 40 marks in total for the sendaway, drop and recall exercise, which is the same for Classes B and C, and, no matter how good the recall, if the dog fails the sendaway there will be no recall to mark. The most important part of teaching the sendaway is to make sure the dog enjoys it. The dog who feels it is being banished for some misdemeanour will skulk away and rarely reach the designated spot but the dog who has been taught the sendaway as a game will race to the box in anticipation of its praise or reward. I know which I'd rather see!

Distant Control

When this exercise is performed well it is a joy to watch. The dog is expected to change position six times, incorporating the stand, sit and down, on command from its handler, who is some distance away. I once saw this exercise performed by a predominantly white Border Collie bitch whose handler gave only visual commands by means of hand signals. Watching this dog go through the six positions faultlessly, in total silence, never taking her eyes from her handler, was beautiful to see. I later saw this same dog

Distant Control: stand.

Distant Control: sit.

performing this exercise for a demonstration with her almost-identical brother. The dogs were standing back to back, facing their respective handlers, and performed distant control exercises simultaneously in total silence – what a spectacle!

Needless to say, competitors do not need to keep silent during this exercise, and either verbal commands or signals are permissible. The dog will be left in a position nominated by the judge and the handler will be sent some distance away to face his or her dog. It is not unusual for the handler

Distant Control: down.

to be given a card with the sequence of the six positions on it. The handler gives each command when instructed by the steward and the dog should immediately take up the new position without moving more than a body length in any direction. The dog will be penalised for any failed position, hesitation or excess movement, and the handler for extra commands or body signals. When teaching this exercise the handler should stay close to the dog until it is 100% reliable – for, once again, if the dog won't change position reliably every time it is asked when the handler is close by there is little hope once the handler leaves the dog. Expert handlers even teach the dog how to move into each position on the spot, with no forward movement at all. Although this is a long process, the result is well worth waiting for.

This dog is confident enough not to be worried
when asked to pick up unusual retrieve items.

EQUIPMENT

You will begin to collect equipment almost as soon as you start training. Your ordinary collar and lead may not be suitable for obedience training and such things as a dumbbell, sendaway markers and scent cloths are basic requirements. Most equipment can be picked up for nothing or made and, despite the exciting array of coloured poles, flashy leads and psychedelic dumbbells on display at shows, it is possible to take part in obedience competitions with very little outlay.

Collar and Lead

The type of collar and lead you use is very much a matter of choice, and what suits one dog and handler may not suit another. In general, the choice of collar will depend on your own method of training. Various check chains, slip collars and nylon half checks are available, as well as the more conventional leather or nylon buckle collar. The lead, however, needs to be strong, soft and lightweight and probably slightly longer than the average pet lead. A split ring in the handle end allows the handler to clip the lead into a circle and wear it around his or her body when it is not in use, ensuring that it will not be put down and lost. In competition, when the dog is on the lead, a heavy or cumbersome lead will impede the dog, and too short a lead will become tight and lose marks far too easily.

Portable Rings

Some handlers carry posts and ropes to rig up a portable ring at their training ground, believing that a dog knows when it is in the ring and should be trained in the same conditions. This may or may not be necessary but will certainly do no harm, and can actually assist the handler in learning the correct speed at which to carry out smooth heelwork at different paces within the confines of the ring.

Dumbbells and Retrieve Objects

Dumbbells are now sold in most pet shops, but there is a tendency of late to make them in luminous colours. I suspect this is more to attract the owners than the dogs, as all dogs are supposed to be colour blind. However, dogs can discern light from dark and, when points depend on the dog marking the dumbbell that has been thrown, I would prefer to see a white dumbbell landing on the green grass. Most dumbbells now are moulded plastic, but there is no reason why you cannot use a wooden dumbbell. Again, I would be inclined to paint the ends white. Make sure the dumbbell

A selection of retrieve items.

fits your dog and clears the ground by enough room to be easily picked up. The best dumbbell to pick up and carry is one that is just wider than the dog's mouth so that it doesn't pinch its lips and has ends big enough to keep it clear of the ground for ease of pick up. If your dumbbell is much too wide for your dog it will encourage the dog to pick it up by one end or the other and carry it unbalanced; if it is too narrow and squashes its lips or cheeks against its teeth the dog may well be unwilling to pick it up at all.

In the higher classes (Test B & C), instead of the dumbbell the retrieve is carried out on the judge's article, so a bag of unusual items is a 'must'. Once you begin to think competitively you will be like a magpie, collecting all manner of things from beer cans to mop heads for your dog to practise retrieve. It is wise to train the dog with all materials and textures, so metal, cloth, plastic and wooden retrieve articles are all essential. The more awkward, heavy or large the items, the better; if your dog can retrieve these items easily, it is much in a better position to cope with whatever the judge might produce.

Examples of Obedience equipment: sendaway markers, ring posts, collar and lead, scent cloths and dumbbell.

Sendaway Markers

Sendaway markers are many and varied and, no matter how great a selection you have, the inventive judge will always come up with a different one. Many top handlers carry a car load of sendaway markers and arrive at a show prepared to practise with a replica of the judge's choice. However, although it's wise to get your dog used to many strange markers, if the exercise has been taught correctly the dog will pay little attention to what the markers are. Some of the more usual and popular markers which you might like to stock up on are: road cones, flower pots, margarine tubs or plastic ice cream cartons, posts (short and long and in various colours including striped), tape for boxes on the ground and rubber car mats.

A variety of sendaway markers.

Scent Cloths

The only other items of equipment necessary are scent cloths, at least some of which should be weighted. These can be bought mail order from some of the training equipment specialists advertising in the dog press or can often be seen at the larger shows on trade stands. It is very difficult for single handlers to prepare their own scent cloths and if they can pair up with a friend, laundering and packaging each other's cloths, this can be a great help. Care must always be taken to ensure that scent cloths are kept sterile, not re-used without washing, and stored in sealed containers in an outhouse or garage between uses.

YOUR FIRST SHOW

If the preceding chapters have not daunted you and you are still intent on trying your luck, perhaps it is time to enter your first show. Assuming that you have had a taste of competition by both watching and competing at exemption shows and matches, the next step is an Open or Championship show. For a first attempt it is probably wise to look for a show close to home, as competing is nerve racking enough without the added stress of a long journey. Pick a show advertised in one of the dog magazines and send for a schedule in good time. When the schedule arrives it will contain an entry form, which must be filled in and sent back with the entry fee before the closing date. Whichever club or society is hosting the show, the entry forms must adhere to a standard format stipulated by The Kennel Club and conform to Kennel Club Regulations. For this reason, apart from club names and logos, they all look much the same and require the same information. The details you fill in on these entry forms must be exactly the same as those submitted to The Kennel Club when your dog was registered. If the dog's parentage and date of birth are not known it is acceptable to enter the name followed by FDU (further details unknown) if this is how the dog is registered at The Kennel Club.

At an Open or Championship show you must enter your dog in the lowest class for which it is eligible and may also enter one other class. Make sure it is clear on the entry form which classes you are entering and check that all details are correct. When you sign the form you are agreeing to abide by KC Rules as well as declaring that your dog is fit to compete and has not been exposed to any contagious diseases. If your dog is exposed to any such disease, becomes ill or comes into season after entries have closed, you must not take it to the show. When all entries have been received the show management will organise a draw for a running order for the first ten dogs in each class (other than Championship C classes where the running order of all competitors is decided by draw) and these ten people will be notified by post before the show. If you are not drawn in the running order it is still necessary to arrive at the show in good time, as all competitors must report to their ringside and book in their class no later than one hour after judging commences.

The show organisers will produce a catalogue of all classes and competitors' names and addresses, and this will be available when you arrive at the show. You will also be given a ring number card to wear while competing, so don't forget your safety pin. Once you have your ring number and your catalogue, go to your ring and book in with the scoreboard steward, who is usually sitting at the table at the ring entrance. If you are not in the running order for the first ten the scoreboard steward may ask you when you would like to work and have a list on which you can write your number in the order. This helps the judge keep the class running smoothly and should be adhered to if at all possible, but stays always take precedence over class work so, if stays clash with a class you are working in, you must let the scoreboard steward know that you are unable to work until later. It is a good idea when you book in to establish what time your stays are and where they will be held. You can write the times on the back of your

The perfect partnership.

ring number so that you don't forget. It is your responsibility to turn up for stays and, if you miss them, you will be disqualified.

Once you know where your rings are, when you are working, and when you must turn up for stays, you can begin to relax. This might be a good time to exercise your dog (there is usually a marked exercise area with facilities for clearing up) and then settle it down with shade and water while you wait your turn. You may find it interesting to watch some of the classes in progress or chat to other competitors, but do not lose track of time or be

Obedience competitions are social occasions where you will meet many like-minded people.

tempted to practise non-stop with your dog. What your dog doesn't know now it isn't going to learn in time, so it is better to let it relax and get used to the show atmosphere.

When it gets near to your turn, get your dog out, give it another chance to visit the exercise area (making sure that you have been yourself!) and make your way to your ring. You will probably have to wait around, as running orders have a habit of going wrong but, when your turn comes, go into the ring and enjoy it. The judge and steward are not monsters. They have all had to start somewhere and they really want to see you do well, so try to relax, help your dog relax and do as the steward tells you. When you have finished your round the judge will probably tell you what marks you have lost and why. Listen to what is said, as this can give you a great indication of what needs improving for next time. Please remember to thank the judge and steward when you leave the ring. They are not paid for their time and without them there would be no show. Much work goes into both planning and directing an obedience class and a little appreciation and courtesy from the competitors can make it all worthwhile. The round is not complete until after the stays and, in Classes A, B and C, until scent has been carried out, so it is often late in the day before you know how you have done overall.

Two friends enjoying their work together.

Whatever the outcome, try to remember that this is a hobby; it is not a life-and-death situation and your survival does not depend on the outcome. To quote an old saying," Tomorrow is another day". The longer you strive for that elusive rosette, the more you will value it when it comes. For your dog it is just a day out that hopefully it will enjoy – make sure that it does not become an ordeal for either of you and, whilst you continue to strive for perfection, remember that your dog, like you, is fallible.

It would be nice to think that this book might inspire a future top handler so, when you make up your first Obedience Champion, drop me a line.

THE KENNEL CLUB

The Kennel Club
Piccadilly
London
W1Y 8AB

THE SCOTTISH KENNEL CLUB

The Scottish Kennel Club
3 Brunswick Place
Edinburgh
EH7 5HP

THE IRISH KENNEL CLUB

The Irish Kennel Club, Ltd
Fottrell House
Unit 36,
Greenmount Office Park
Dublin 6 W

DOG TRAINING WEEKLY

Dog Training Weekly
4-5 Feidr Castell Business Park
Fishguard
Dyfed
SA65 9BB

PRO DOGS

PRO Dogs National Charity
Rocky Bank
4 New Road
Ditton
Aylesford
Kent
ME20 6AD